CONTENTS

Introduction

CATALONIAN SONG 2

RUMORES DE LA CALETA 4

ROMANCE 10

T0050932

CATALONIAN SONG

Arranged by
JACK MARSHALL

Anonymous

VII
II
1/2 II
I
II
VII
1/2 II
1/2 II
2/3 IV
II
p
harm.
XII
I
XII
VII
harm.
harm.
harm. VII

RUMORES DE LA CALETA

Malagueña

Arranged by
CHRISTOPHER PARKENING

I. ALBENIZ

2/3 IX
a m i
p
1/2 V
1/2 V

V
p
m i a m
Lento
1/2 IX
ff
1/2 X
harm.
VIII
V

III
V
V
rit.
III
I
Adagio
ad lib
Cadenza Lento
Riten
Allegro
p
i m a
i m

p p p
2/3 IX
1/2 V

1/2 V
p
p
Lento

ROMANCE

Arranged by
JACK MARSHALL

Anonymous

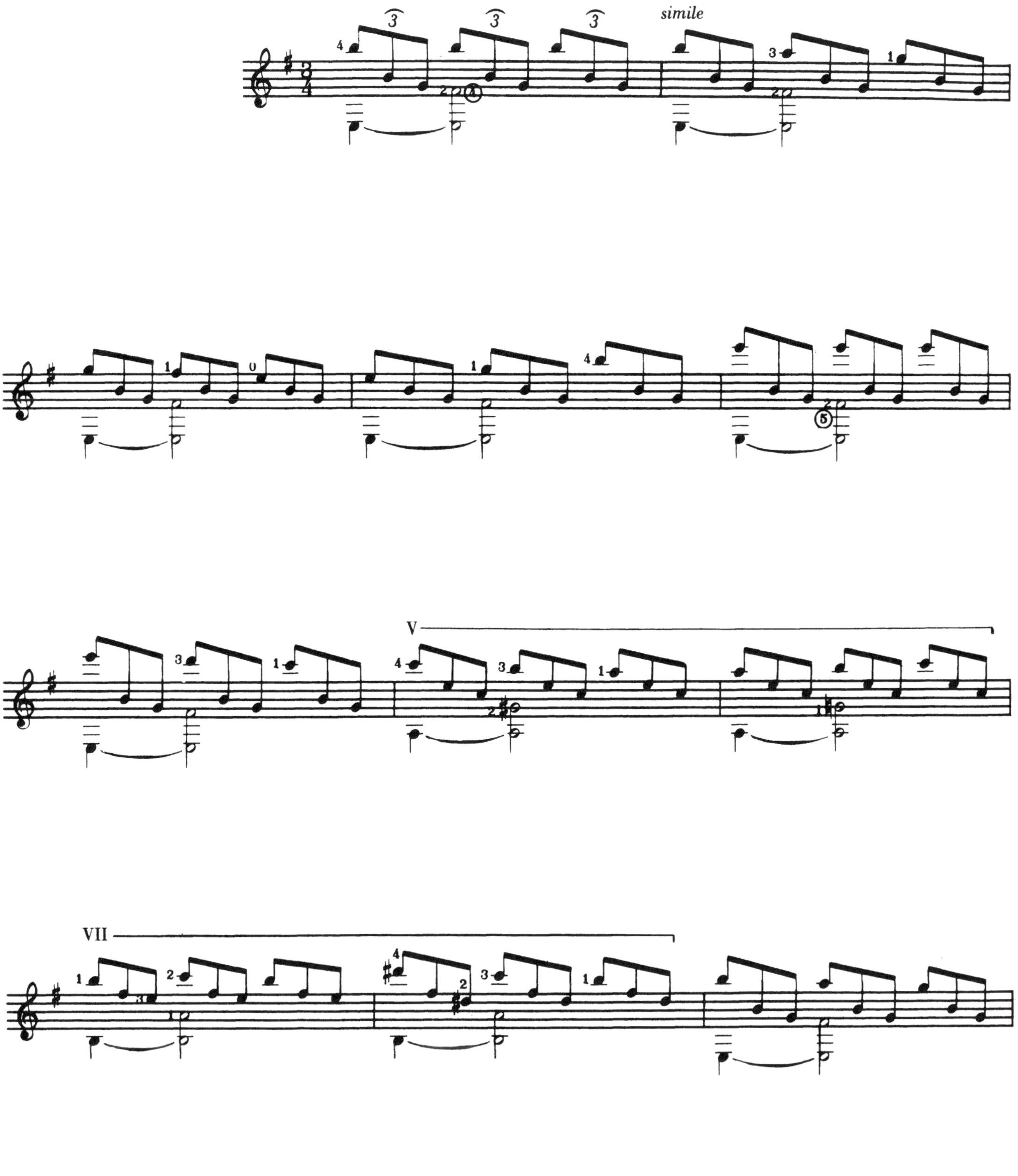

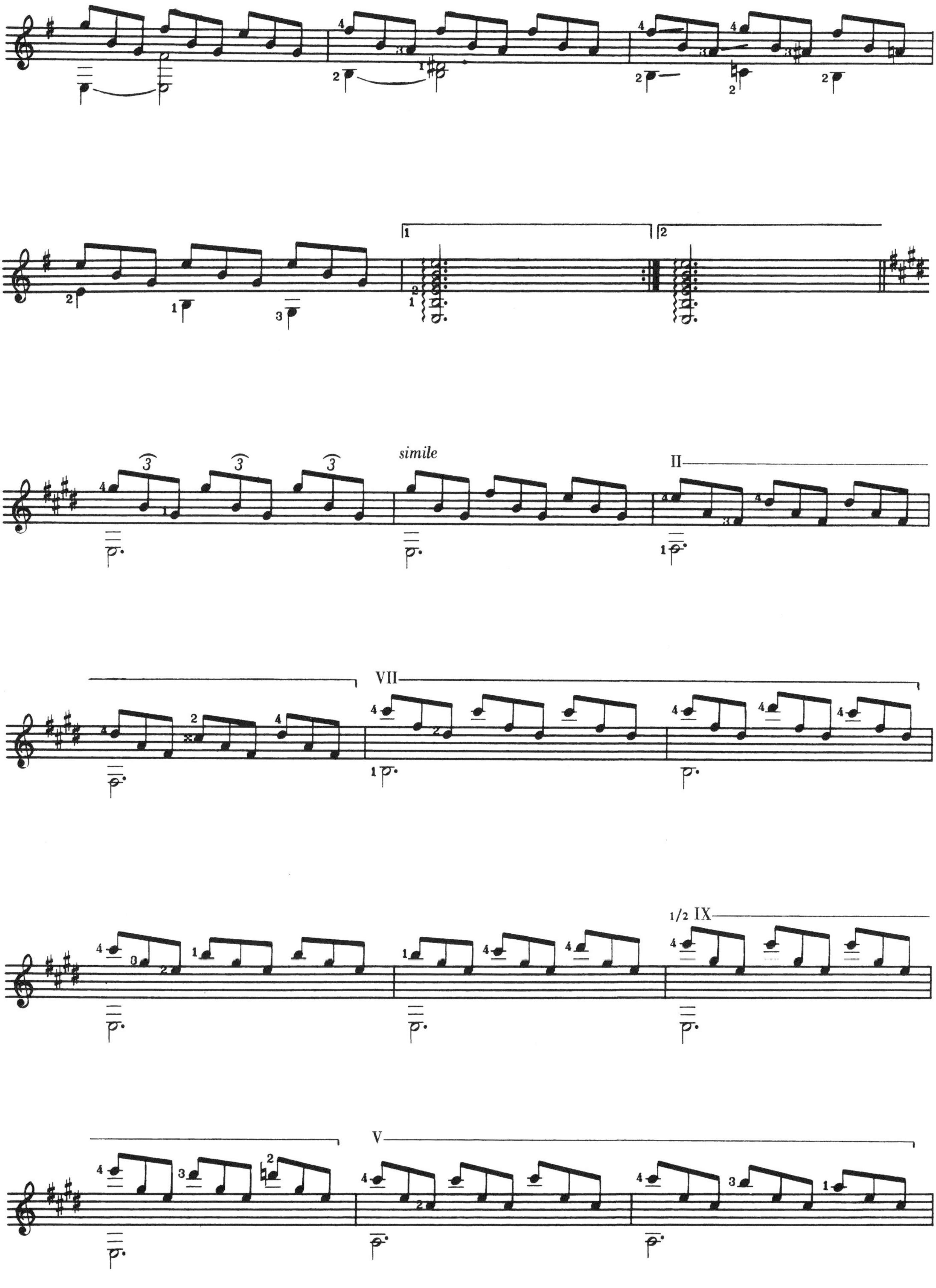
simile
II
VII
1/2 IX
V

II
simile
VII
VI
2/3 V
VII